My Florida Alphabet

My Florida
Alphabet

Russell W. Johnson and Annie P. Johnson

Illustrations by John Hume

Pineapple Press, Inc.
Sarasota, Florida

We dedicate this book to our mothers, whose advice has always seemed to pay off:
"Clean your room!" . . . "Get a job!" . . . "Write a book!"

Inquiries should be addressed to:

Pineapple Press, Inc.
P.O. Box 3889
Sarasota, Florida 34230

www.pineapplepress.com

Library of Congress Cataloging in Publication Data
Johnson, Russell W., 1958-
  My Florida alphabet / Russell W. Johnson and Annie P. Johnson. — 1st ed.
    p. cm.
  ISBN 978-1-56164-392-9 (hardback : alk. paper)
  1. Florida—Juvenile literature. 2. English language—Alphabet—Juvenile literature. I. Johnson, Annie, 1942- II. Title.
  F311.3.J64 2007
  975.9—dc22

                                        2006035339

First Edition
10 9 8 7 6 5 4 3 2 1

Printed in China

Introduction

My Florida Alphabet is not just another alphabet. Join Big Al, the tugboat, as he highlights various animals, characters, places, weather conditions, and such, that make the Sunshine State a great place to call home . . . or visit! So sing along, while performing the gestures for each letter.

Research continues to prove that adding movement, music, and rhythm while teaching a concept facilitates learning. We've seen it happen in our classroom, where we have used this approach for many years. Note that the song uses the *sound* of each letter as a preparation for reading. Teachers and parents will enjoy watching children learn their letter sounds as they see, hear, sing, and pantomime gestures for each letter.

The catchy "My Florida Alphabet" song, performed by elementary students, is easily learned, but not easily forgotten. **A CD with the song is included inside the back cover.**

Join Evy and Bel as they demonstrate each gesture through pictures. A written explanation of each gesture is included for clarification.

We've included reproducible "finger cards" for each letter at the back of the book. These can be used as flash cards or to create simple words through sound combinations (e.g., at, up, is, bag, etc.).

The variety of subjects used for the letters can also be a launching pad for studies in science and social studies.

So . . . hop aboard with Big Al as he navigates his 26 barges through Florida . . . and your child's imagination!

— Russ and Annie Johnson

My Florida Alphabet

Intro   I love my alphabet, I love my state.
And I love learning . . . man, it's great!
Put the three together, what do you get?
You get an alphabet that just won't quit!

Aa	alligator	
Bb	boat	
Cc	conch shells (they don't float)	
Dd	dolphin swimming oh so fast	
Ee	Everglades, sea of grass	(PAUSE)

Ff	fishin' in the	
Gg	Gulf	
Hh	heron with a fish in its mouth	
Ii	itch from mosquito bites	
Jj	jellyfish (what a sight)	

(CHORUS)

Kk	Key deer (almost extinct)	
Ll	lobster (tasty, I think)	
Mm	manatee, gentle and slow	
Nn	Naples (where the old folks go)	(PAUSE)

Oo	Osceola, Indian chief	
Pp	Pennekamp, coral reef	
Qq	quarter moon, time to sail	
Rr	raccoon with a long, ringed tail	

Ss	suntan on a winter's day
Tt	turtle floating on the bay
Uu	umbrella, always in reach
Vv	"varoom" at Daytona Beach

(PAUSE)

Ww	waterspout off the coast
Xx	extra juicy clams you can roast
Yy	yellowfly, "ouch, that stings!"
Zz	Zephyrhills, famous springs

CHORUS
Singin' my . . . Florida Alphabet
Stick around, you ain't heard nothin' yet
My . . . Florida Alphabet, sing along with me

Aa

alligator

Alligator — With arms straight and elbows locked, open wide and close.

Bb
boat

Boat — Mimic steering a boat (similar to car); twist left and right repeatedly.

Cc
conch shells

Conch shells — Place shell to ear and listen; then toss back in the ocean.

Dd

dolphin

Dolphin — Join hands, thumbs up, and dive, dive, dive.

Ee

Everglades

Everglades —With arms above head, sway left-right-left-right
(like grass in moving water).

Ff
fishin'

Fishin' —Hold a fishing pole and reel in the big one!

Gg
Gulf

Gulf — Interlock fingers and create a fluid wave effect by
up and down motion of hands and arms.

Hh

heron

Heron — One hand creates a beak while other hand (fish) is inserted into beak.

Ii

itch

Itch — Scratch those mosquito bites!

Jj

jellyfish

Jellyfish — Look surprised at seeing a jellyfish; step back and point towards the ground.

Kk

Key deer

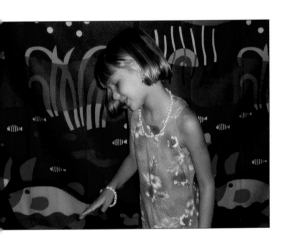

Key deer —Kneel down on one knee and pet this miniature deer gently.

L l

lobster

Lobster — With arms out to sides, elbows bent with hands upward, open and close claws.

Mm

manatee

Manatee — With palms together at waist level, the manatee swims upward in a fluid motion.

Nn

Naples

Naples — Role-play an older person. One hand holds cane, other holds aching back.

Oo

Osceola

Osceola —Stand tall and proud with folded arms and a serious look.

Pp
Pennekamp

Pennekamp — Place a snorkeling mask on face; then look left and right for sea life.

Qq

quarter moon

Quarter moon —Reach up, grab sail rope, and pull down, hand over hand.

Rr

raccoon

Raccoon — Extend either arm to resemble a long tail; wave back and forth.

Ss

suntan

 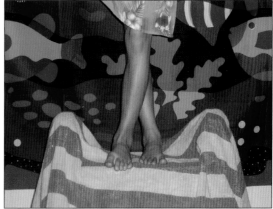

Suntan —While standing, cross legs, place hands behind head, and close eyes (vertical sunbathing!).

Tt

turtle

Turtle —With arms bent at elbows and hands near neck to resemble flippers, flip repeatedly.

Uu

umbrella

Umbrella — Hold umbrella pointing downward, then lift upward and open it while looking up.

Vv

"varoom"

Varoom —With a look of excitement, point at a car and follow it with finger as it speeds by.

Ww

waterspout

Waterspout —Spiral pointer finger upward.

Xx

eXtra juicy clams

Extra juicy clams —Cup hands together (one on top, one on bottom) and open and close.

*NOTE: The X makes a "ks" sound. It is difficult to hear in the word "extra." We suggest you teach the "ks" sound in isolation.

Yy

yellowfly

Yellowfly — Hold arm out to side and *gently* slap that nasty yellowfly.

Zz

Zephyrhills

Zephyrhills —Hold bottled water in front of body; then unscrew the cap and drink.

Finger Cards

The following pages are "finger cards," one for each letter. You can reproduce them to use for further teaching of letter sounds.

Use them as flash cards. Show a card and ask, "What sound does it make? What letter is this? What are some words that start with this sound?"

You can use them to create simple words through sound combinations (e.g., at, up, is, bag, cat, lot, and, hat, dig, etc.).

Aa

Bb

Cc

Dd

Ee

Ff

Gg

Hh

Ii

Jj

Kk

Ll

Mm

Nn

Oo

Pp

Qq

Rr

S s

T t

U u

V v

W w

X x

Y y

Z z

If you enjoyed reading this book, here are some other books from Pineapple Press on related topics. Ask your local bookseller for our books. For a complete catalog, write to Pineapple Press, P.O. Box 3889, Sarasota, FL 34230 or call 1-800-PINEAPL (746-3275). Or visit our website at www.pineapplepress.com.

Florida A to Z by Susan Jane Ryan. Crammed into colorful illustration and photo collages—one for each letter of the alphabet—are almost two hundred facts about Florida personalities, history, geography, nature, and culture. Full color; for readers ages 8–12.

Those Outrageous Owls by Laura Wyatt. *Those Terrific Turtles* by Sarah Cussen. *Those Amazing Alligators* by Kathy Feeney. *Those Excellent Eagles* by Jan Lee Wicker. *Those Peculiar Pelicans* by Sarah Cussen. *Those Funny Flamingos* by Jan Lee Wicker. Each of these books contains 20 questions and answers about these fascinating creatures. Illustrated by Steve Weaver. Ages 5–9.

The Old Man and the C by Carole Jean Tremblay. Illustrated by Angela Donato. In his trusty rowboat, the *C-Worthy,* Charlie sets out to win the Fish-or-Cut-Bait Fishing Tournament. What he catches is a surprise to everyone. A quest for a big fish turns into an amusing adventure involving a bad case of the hiccups. Ages 6–10.

Esmeralda and the Enchanted Pond by Susan Ryan. Delightful, full-color illustrations highlight the story of Esmeralda and her father, who visit a Florida forest during all four seasons and discover that there's a scientific explanation for everything that seems magical. An illustrated activity guide that conforms to the Sunshine State Standards is also available. Ages 8–11.

Patchwork: Seminole and Miccosukee Art and Activities by Dorothy Downs. Learn about the history of the Seminole and Miccosukee people, and how they do their crafts. Learn how to make your very own patchwork and doll, just like the Seminoles and Miccosukees—using colored paper and glue instead of fabric and a sewing machine. Ages 9–12.

Legends of the Seminoles by Betty Mae Jumper. This collection of rich spoken tales—written down for the first time—impart valuable lessons about living in harmony with nature and about why the world is the way it is. Each story is illustrated with an original painting by Guy LaBree. All ages.

Florida Lighthouses for Kids by Elinor De Wire. Details the history and lore of Florida's thirty-three lighthouses: who built them, who's looked after them, what they've been through, and how they operate. Ages 9 up.